GO FACTS WONDERS

Modern Wonders

Blake
EDUCATION
Better ways to learn

Modern Wonders

contents

Go Facts — Wonders
Modern Wonders

ISBN: 978-1-74164-533-0

Copyright © 2009 Blake Publishing
Published by Blake Education Pty Ltd
ABN 50 074 266 023
108 Main Rd
Clayton South VIC 3169

Phone (03) 9558 4433
Fax (03) 9558 5433

Email: info@blake.com.au
Web: www.blake.com.au

Written by Nicolas Brasch and Mark Stafford
Publisher: Katy Pike
Editor: Emma Waterhouse
Photo research: Anna Di Losa
Design and layout by The Modern Art Production Group
Printed by Tara TPS

Image credits: pp 6(br), 7(tl) (b), 13(bl), 19(b), 20(br), 21(t), 23(m), 26(br),
27(tr) (b), 28(bl)–Photolibrary; p 29(tr)–Corbis

Modern Wonders

Modern wonders are special buildings and monuments that are significant because of their size, beauty, historical and cultural worth.

What people have made

It is hard to define what makes something a modern wonder. The Christ the Redeemer Statue in Brazil is not the largest in the world, but its setting on top of a mountain is spectacular. Kinkaku-ji is not the most important temple for Japanese Buddhists, but it is covered in pure gold and has an amazing history.

A construction like the North Sea Protection Works is not considered beautiful, but its role in the lives of Dutch people is vital. The Burj Dubai tower in the Middle East is a wonder because of its height — it is almost twice as tall as the next highest building in the world. The Sistine Chapel is a single room, but it holds some of the most beautiful and **iconic** paintings ever produced.

All these buildings and monuments draw millions of visitors every year to marvel at what other people have made.

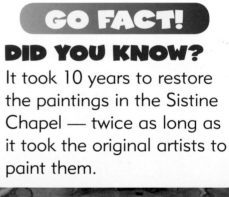

GO FACT!
DID YOU KNOW?

It took 10 years to restore the paintings in the Sistine Chapel — twice as long as it took the original artists to paint them.

Modern Wonders around the World

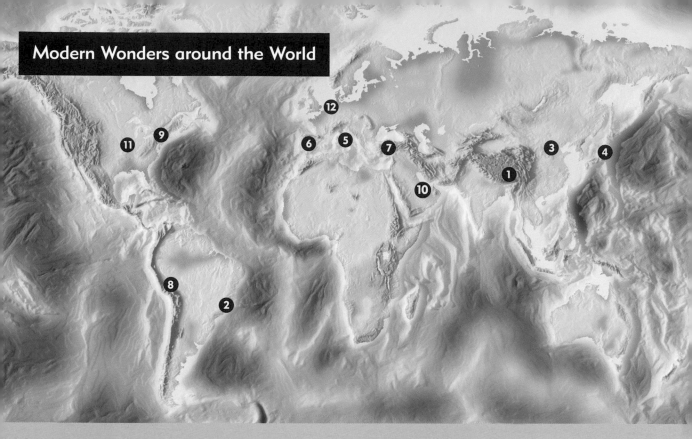

 **Potala Palace**
Tibet

 Christ the Redeemer Statue
Brazil

 **Forbidden City**
China

 **Kinkaku-ji**
Japan

 **Sistine Chapel**
Italy

 **Alhambra**
Spain

 **Hagia Sophia**
Turkey

 **Machu Picchu**
Peru

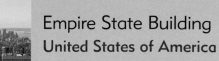 **Empire State Building**
United States of America

 Burj Dubai
United Arab Emirates

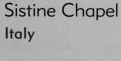 **Gateway Arch**
United States of America

 **North Sea Protection Works**
Netherlands

5

Potala Palace

The Potala Palace is in the city of Lhasa, Tibet. It is the highest palace in the world and the former home of the **Dalai Lamas**.

Red and white

Potala Palace stands 3 500 metres above sea level and was completed in 1694. It has more than 1 000 rooms and sloping stone walls that are about 3 metres thick.

The central part of the palace is the Red Palace. It contains the main halls, libraries, chapels and shrines of past Dalai Lamas, who were spiritual leaders of Tibet and teachers of Buddhism. There has been a succession of 14 Dalai Lamas since the 14th century. The 14th Dalai Lama, Tenzin Gyatso, currently lives in India.

The Red Palace also holds the sacred stupas, which are the tombs of eight Dalai Lamas. The stupa of the Fifth Dalai Lama is made out of wood and covered in 4 tonnes of gold and 18 680 pearls and jewels.

The surrounding White Palace makes up the living quarters of the Dalai Lamas.

Politics and rebellion

For over 300 years, the Dalai Lamas lived in the Potala Palace. In 1959, there was an uprising against the Chinese rulers of Tibet. The 14th Dalai Lama fled to India, and the Potala Palace was converted into a museum.

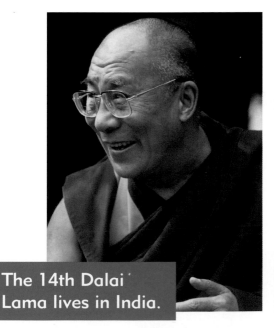

The 14th Dalai Lama lives in India.

A **monk** at the Potala Palace.

There are eight golden stupas at the Potala Palace. Each one is the tomb of a past Dalai Lama.

the Red palace

the White palace

HIGHEST
The Potala Palace is about 117 metres tall.

Christ the Redeemer Statue

The Christ the Redeemer Statue stands above Rio de Janeiro in Brazil. It has become a symbol of the city below and the faith of its people.

Size and scope

In 1921, the leaders of the Catholic Church in Brazil decided that the city of Rio de Janeiro should have a statue of Jesus Christ. They chose to build the statue on top of the Corcovado mountain.

Brazilians, Heitor da Silva Costa and Carlos Oswald, designed the statue and the French sculptor, Paul Landowski, sculpted it. People donated money for 10 years to pay for the building costs. It took nine years for workers to construct the statue. It was completed on 12 October 1931.

The Corcovado mountain is over 700 metres high.

Construction

The designers built different models of the Christ the Redeemer statue before they agreed on the design. Trains transported the builders and building materials to the top of the mountain. The statue is made out of concrete. It is coated with **soapstone** which is resistant to sun, wind and rain.

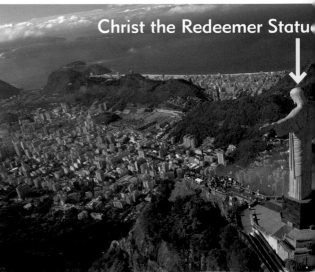

Christ the Redeemer Statue

The Dimensions of the Statue

Arm span: 30 metres

Height: 38 metres

Weight: over 600 tonnes

Forbidden City

The Forbidden City lies in the centre of Beijing, China. With 900 buildings and almost 10 000 rooms, it is the largest palace complex in the world.

For the Emperor

The Forbidden City was built from 1406–1420 AD for the Emperor and his family and servants. It was called the Forbidden City because no-one could enter or leave the city without the Emperor's permission. The Emperor and his family lived in the Inner Court. In the Outer Court, three halls sit on top of a white marble terrace, the largest of which is the Hall of Supreme Harmony. Ceremonies, such as **coronations** and royal weddings were held here.

It took 100 000 artists and one million workers 14 years to build the Forbidden City. It is made from timber, marble, stone and bricks made of sticky rice and egg whites. The palace complex is surrounded by a 10 metre-high wall and a 6 metre-deep moat. A tower sits in each corner of the wall. To protect the buildings from catching on fire, giant bronze cauldrons filled with water were placed throughout the palace.

The last emperor

The Forbidden City was the home of 24 emperors. The last emperor of China left the palace in 1924. Today, the Forbidden City houses the Palace Museum. It holds over one million paintings, statues and pieces of jewellery.

GO FACT!

DID YOU KNOW?

Yellow is the colour of the Emperor, so almost all roofs in the Forbidden City have yellow tiles.

The Hall of Supreme Harmony is the largest wooden structure in China.

The Palace Museum contains almost 50 000 paintings.

Two bronze lion statues guard the Gate of Supreme Harmony.

Kinkaku-ji

Covered in pure gold, Kinkaku-ji in Kyoto is one of the most picturesque examples of Japanese culture.

Kinkaku-ji is also known as the Temple of the Golden Pavilion or Deer Park Temple. The **Shogun** Yoshimitsu built Kinkaku-ji as part of his retirement estate in 1398. After his death in 1408, the grounds were turned into a temple.

Like many structures in Kyoto, Kinkaku-ji has been completely rebuilt. It survived fires, wars and earthquakes for centuries, but was burnt to the ground in 1950 when a monk set fire to it.

Kinkaku-ji contains sacred statues of the Buddha.

Mixing styles

The pavilion and its pond were designed to look like a Buddhist paradise. The pond has lotus plants, which are symbols of truth. Stones and islands represent the eight oceans and nine mountains of the Buddhist creation story.

Kinkaku-ji has three floors, each in a different style. The first floor was used as a hall for welcoming guests. The second floor was built in the style of **samurai** houses. This is where Yoshimitsu held meetings with guests. The top floor, only a few square metres, was used for private meetings with friends and tea ceremonies.

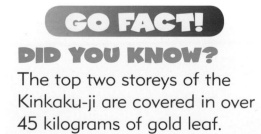

GO FACT!

DID YOU KNOW?

The top two storeys of the Kinkaku-ji are covered in over 45 kilograms of gold leaf.

The Kinkaku-ji Temple

More than 1.5 million people visit Kinkaku-ji every year.

A statue of a **phoenix** sits on the roof of the Kinkaku-ji.

This is a painting of a shogun. Different shoguns ruled Japan from 794–1868.

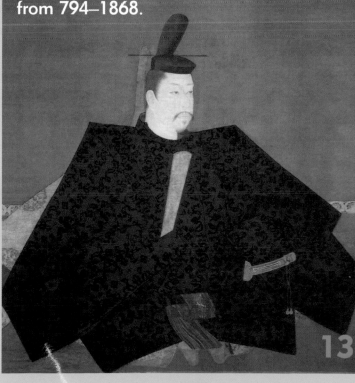

13

Sistine Chapel

The Sistine Chapel in Rome, Italy, contains some of the most famous and valuable artworks in the world.

Painting in plaster

In the 1470s, **Pope** Sixtus IV built the Sistine Chapel to host ceremonies and functions of the church. One of the major functions of the Sistine Chapel is as a venue for the election of each pope.

The chapel is the same size as the Temple of Solomon, described in the Bible. When the chapel was finished, the pope **commissioned** artists, such as Botticelli, Rosselli and Perugino, to paint frescoes on the walls of the chapel. Frescoes are painted onto wet plaster — when the plaster dries, the painting is part of the wall. They painted scenes from the Bible and portraits of the popes.

Michelangelo at work

In 1508, Pope Julius II commissioned Michelangelo to paint ceiling frescoes in the chapel. Michelangelo painted while lying on his back, on top of scaffolding. He did this almost every day for more than four years. His series of nine paintings show *God's Creation of the World*, *God's Relationship with Mankind*, and *Mankind's Fall from God's Grace*.

Almost 30 years later, Michelangelo was asked to paint the **altar** wall. The work is called *The Last Judgement*.

Michelangelo's painting of Daniel, before and after restoration that began in 1984.

One of the most famous paintings is called *The Creation of Adam*. In the painting, the hand of God touches Adam to give him life.

a portrait of Michelangelo

Michelangelo painted more than 300 figures on the ceiling of the Sistine Chapel.

Alhambra

The Alhambra is a palace and fortress in Granada, Spain. It contains some of Spain's most beautiful Islamic art and architecture.

Seat of sultans

In the 8th century, nearly all of Spain was conquered by **Muslim** armies from North Africa. The Alhambra was built in the 9th century. High on a terrace over the city, it protected the people below from invaders.

Towards the end of Muslim rule in Spain, it was extended and restored by Yusuf I and his son Muhammed V, Sultan of Granada. Christian armies from the north conquered Granada in 1492, although the Alhambra was never attacked.

Intricate art

There are three main parts to the Alhambra.

The Royal Palace is a collection of residences, corridors, meeting rooms and courtyards. They are richly decorated with coloured tiles and **intricate** stone carvings. Many of the decorations are arabesques, which are detailed repeating patterns based on flowers, leaves and branches, often twisted together.

The fortress of Alcazaba is a series of walls and towers. It is the oldest part of the Alhambra. The Generalife is a villa. Its gardens contain many fountains, including one that runs down the rails of a staircase.

an arabesque carved in plaster

At the centre of the Court of Lions is a basin sitting on 12 white marble lions.

the Gardens of Generalife

DID YOU KNOW?

The Alhambra has not only inspired architects and artists around the world, but novelists, composers, musicians and film makers, including Philippa Gregory's historical fiction novel, *The Constant Princess*.

The name 'Alhambra' comes from an Arabic word meaning 'red'. The Alhambra was made out of red clay.

Hagia Sophia

The Hagia Sophia is a museum in Istanbul, Turkey. But for almost 1 000 years, it was the largest church in the world. It is famous for its massive dome and **Byzantine** architecture.

A church like no other

Hagia Sophia was built from 532–537 AD by Emperor Justinian I. He wanted to build a church that was different from any other. The Emperor brought precious stones from all over his empire for the building.

A troubled history

The original dome collapsed after an earthquake in 558 AD. It was rebuilt but collapsed again in 563 AD. Earthquakes in 989 AD and 1346 AD also damaged parts of the building.

In 1453, the **Ottoman Turks** conquered Constantinople and converted Hagia Sophia into a **mosque**. Four minarets (spires), a regular feature of mosques, were built around the mosque. Hagia Sophia was the main mosque of Istanbul for almost 500 years until it became a museum in 1935.

Colour and light

The huge dome is 55 metres above the ground. There are 40 arched windows underneath it, which flood the interior with light. The interior is covered with green, white and purple marble and gold mosaics.

a mosaic of the Virgin Mary and Child

Hagia Sophia was the model for many other mosques.

FIRST

The Byzantine architects were the first to succeed in building a round dome on the top of a rectangular building. They placed the dome on massive columns instead of walls.

19

Machu Picchu

Machu Picchu is the ruins of a city in Peru. In a spectacular mountain setting, it is an excellent example of the **Inca** Empire at its peak.

Left alone

Machu Picchu is sometimes called the Lost City of the Incas. The Incas built Machu Picchu around 1450 AD. But only 100 years later, the city was deserted. Most of the approximately 1 200 people that lived there probably died of smallpox, a disease introduced by the Spanish.

The city was never found by the invading Spanish. It lay undisturbed for almost 500 years.

Built without mortar

Machu Picchu was most likely a royal and religious **refuge**. It had approximately 200 buildings. They were mainly houses, but also temples, storage and other public buildings. The houses had steep, thatched roofs but few windows.

Most buildings were made of granite blocks, cut with bronze or stone tools and smoothed with sand. Many of the blocks weigh at least 50 tonnes. The blocks fit together perfectly without **mortar**, although none are the same size.

The Incas planted crops, such as potatoes and corn, in terraces.

FIRST

One of the first people to discover Machu Picchu was Hiram Bingham, an archaeologist from Yale University, USA, in 1911.

More than 2 000 tourists visit Machu Picchu every day.

This is the Intihuatana stone. Historians believe the Incas used the stone like a clock to tell the time.

This place is called the Temple of the Sun.

Skyscrapers

Modern skyscrapers are the tallest buildings in the world. Modern building materials make it possible to build such tall structures.

Space and steel

Developers built the first modern skyscrapers in New York City during the 1800s. The population in the city was growing rapidly, but because it sat on an island, there wasn't much space for new buildings. The only way to make room was to build taller buildings.

New York City developers competed among themselves. Each new major building claimed the title of world's tallest. In 1930, the Chrysler Building (319 metres) was completed and the Empire State Building (381 metres) followed soon after in 1931. The World Trade Center towers (415–417 metres) became the world's tallest buildings in 1972, before the title passed to Chicago, when the Sears Tower (442 metres) was built in 1974.

Now and tomorrow

In 2003, Taipei became the first country outside the USA to build the tallest skyscraper in the world, Taipei 101. The tallest skyscrapers now stand, or are being built, in the Middle East. There are also plans for future "supertall towers", with heights of more than one kilometre.

FIRST

The first skyscraper in the world was probably the ten-storey Home Insurance Company Building, in Chicago. It was built in 1885 and demolished in 1931.

It took 3 000 workers only 410 days to build the Empire State Building.

A worker tightens bolts on the Empire State Building during construction. The Chrysler Building is in the background.

The Petronas Twin Towers in Kuala Lumpur, Malaysia, are the tallest twin towers in the world.

The World Trade Center towers were destroyed in 2001.

Taipei 101

Burj Dubai

Burj Dubai is a modern skyscraper in the United Arab Emirates. It is the tallest human-made structure in the world.

Burj Dubai is 818 metres tall. The tower contains apartments, hotels, shops, swimming pools and offices. It has an observation deck on level 124.

More than 7 000 people, mainly from India, Pakistan, Bangladesh, China and the Philippines, worked to build Burj Dubai.

Designing for height

The tower's shape was inspired by a desert flower and Islamic architecture. The architects invented a new structural system to build the tower. They had to consider differences between ground level and the building's final height — the temperature can vary up to 8°C, humidity can differ by 30% and the air can be 10% thinner.

It is the first time since the Great Pyramid of Giza that the world's tallest building has been in the Middle East.

Wind engineering

Viewed from above, Burj Dubai is a Y shape. However, its shape changes at different heights. This reduces the wind forces on the tower. The builders also used a special **sealant** to bond the glass walls and metal frames.

GO FACT!

DID YOU KNOW?

Burj Dubai has 54 elevators. The fastest reaches 35 kilometres per hour. The trip to the top takes about 55 seconds.

A Comparison of Different Skyscrapers

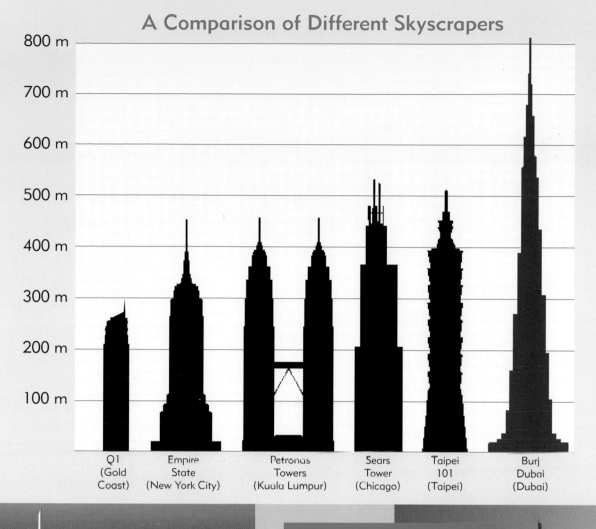

Q1 (Gold Coast)	Empire State (New York City)	Petronas Towers (Kuala Lumpur)	Sears Tower (Chicago)	Taipei 101 (Taipei)	Burj Dubai (Dubai)

The Burj Dubai tower's observation deck is 442 metres above ground — the highest publicly accessible observation deck in the world.

The Burj Al Arab is also in Dubai. At 321 metres, it is the second tallest hotel in the world.

Gateway Arch

The Gateway Arch in St Louis, USA, is an architectural wonder and the tallest monument in the country.

Competition

In 1947, there was a competition to design a monument to honour former US President, Thomas Jefferson. The monument was also to celebrate the westward expansion of **pioneers** across the United States during the 19th century.

The competition judges considered different designs, such as an **obelisk**, a box and a dome. They chose an arch, designed by Finnish-American architect, Eero Saarinen.

The finished product

The Gateway Arch was built from 1963–1965. It is 192 metres tall and 192 metres from one edge of the base to the other. Each leg was built at the same time. To make sure the legs would meet at the top, the building work had to be accurate to within 0.39 millimetres.

The arch can sway up to 23 centimetres each way, if winds reach 240 kilometres per hour. The arch's usual sway is 1.3 centimetres each way.

People can visit the top of the arch. Rather than climb the 1 076 stairs, there is a tram system that carries people to the top.

Workers used about 900 tonnes of stainless steel to build the Gateway Arch.

DID YOU KNOW?

The arch is a catenary curve, which is the shape a free-hanging chain takes when held at both ends.

a painting of pioneers in the 1800s

About one million visitors travel to the observation deck at the top of the Gateway Arch each year.

North Sea Protection Works

The North Sea Protection Works is a 30 kilometre-long series of dams along the coast of the Netherlands. It is one of the most extensive engineering projects in the world and has made millions of Dutch people much safer.

Lowlands

The North Sea Protection Works protect the southern Netherlands from floods. The name 'Netherlands' comes from a Dutch word that means 'low countries'. Much of the country lies below sea level. After heavy storms, the waters of the North Sea rise and threaten the country with flooding.

The single largest part of the North Sea Protection works is the Oosterschelde storm-surge barrier. It is three kilometres long.

In 1953, a severe flood breached Netherlands' **dikes**. It killed almost 2 000 people and left tens of thousands of people homeless. Before the flood, the government had begun to improve the country's protection against floods — after the flood, work became much faster.

Water control

From 1958–1997, workers built barriers, dams, **locks**, **sluices** and dikes. A storm barrier looks like a dam but its wall can be opened and closed to control water flow. Existing dams and dikes were also strengthened.

The North Sea Protection Works has more than 16 500 km of dikes and 300 structures. This part of the Netherlands is now much safer.

The Oosterschelde dam has sliding steel gates. The gates weigh between 300–500 metric tonnes. They can be raised and lowered to control the flow of water.

In 1953, the North Sea Flood destroyed over 4 000 buildings and forced 70 000 people to evacuate.

GO FACT!

DID YOU KNOW?

Some dams have fish tunnels, which allow fish to swim freely between the North Sea and the Netherlands' rivers.

a satellite photograph of the south coast of the Netherlands

Dam

Dam

Canal

Bridge

Oosterschelde storm-surge barrier

Timeline

Modern Wonders

Hagia Sophia
532 AD

Potala Palace
637

Alhambra
800s

Kinkaku-ji
1397

Forbidden City
1406

Macchu Picchu
1450 AD

Sistine Chapel
1470s

Skyscrapers
1880s

Christ the Redeemer Statue
1931

Burj Dubai
2004

Other events around the same time

500 AD – The Maya city of Uxmal was founded in the state of the Yucatan.

636 AD – The Muslims conquerd Persia.

800s AD – Charles the Great is crowned Emperor in Rome, marking the start of the Holy Roman Empire.

1399 – Henry IV became King of England.

1406 – James I became King of Scotland.

1460 – The first Portuguese explorers reached the coast of what is now known as Sierra Leone, West Africa.

1485 – Forty years of civil war in England, known as the War of the Roses, ended.

1880s – First edition of Oxford English Dictionary was published; Arthur Conan Doyle published his first Sherlock Holmes tale; Ned Kelly was hanged in Melbourne Gaol.

1931 – Australia got its first Australian-born Governor-General.

2004 – NASA's exploration robot, Spirit, landed on Mars.

Glossary

altar a raised, typically flat-topped structure, such as a table, where religious ceremonies are performed

Byzantine relating to the eastern part of the late Roman Empire

commissioned a job or task given to a person or a group, to produce a particular product or piece of work

coronation the ceremony or act of crowning a monarch

Dalai Lama the spiritual leader of the Tibetan Buddhists

dike a barrier built along the shore of the sea, lake or river to prevent flooding

Inca Native South American people whose empire, based in Peru, lasted from the 12th–mid 16th century

intricate something that contains many details that are combined in a complex or skilful way

iconic relating to or characteristic of something famous or religious

lock part of a canal where the water level can be raised or lowered to allow boats to pass through two parts of the waterway

monk a man who goes to live in a religious community to devote himself to prayer and contemplation

mosque a building in which Muslims worship

mortar a material that binds rocks and stones together

Muslim/Moslem a follower of Islam/the Islamic religion

obelisk a tall, four-sided shaft of stone

Ottoman Turks people who lived within the Ottoman Empire (now Turkey)

phoenix a bird from ancient mythology

pioneers the first people to explore a territory

pope the head of the Catholic Church

refuge a place that offers protection or safe shelter

samurai a class of Japanese warriors between the 11th and the 19th centuries

sealant a substance used to seal something, eg by filling gaps

shogun a rank of Japanese military commander who ruled the country under the Emperor between 1192–1867

sluice an artificial channel for water to flow through; controlled by a gate

soapstone a soft stone that is either dark grey or green

Index